P9-DLZ-211

PRESIDENTS OF THE U.S.A.

GEORGE BUSH
OUR FORTY-FIRST PRESIDENT

by Sandra Francis

THE CHILD'S WORLD ®

Published in the United States of America

The Child's World®
1980 Lookout Drive • Mankato, MN 56003-1705
800-599-READ • www.childsworld.com

Acknowledgments
The Child's World®: Mary Berendes, Publishing Director

The Creative Spark: Mary McGavic, Project Director and Page Production;
Shari Joffe, Editorial Director; Deborah Goodsite, Photo Research

The Design Lab: Kathleen Petelinsek, Design

Content Adviser: David R. Smith, Adjunct Assistant Professor of History,
University of Michigan–Ann Arbor

Photos
Cover and page 3: William Coupon/Corbis

Interior: Associated Press Images: 16, 34 (AP Photo), 19 (The Daily Oklahoman,
Steve Sisney), 23 (Pat Wellenbach), 26 (Scott Applewhite), 31 (Ron Edmonds),
37 (Cheryl Gerber); Corbis: 27 (Ron Sachs/CNP), 28 (Martin H. Simon), 29
(Bettmann), 30 (Wolfgang Kumm/dpa), 33 (Georges de Keerle/Sygma); George
Bush Presidential Library and Museum: 5, 8 and 38, 9, 10, 11, 13, 14, 15, 18,
25; Getty Images: 4, 17, 22, 24 (Getty); 7 and 39, 32 and 39, 36 (AFP); The
Image Works: 12 (George Bush Presidential Library), 21 (Topham), 35 (Pool
/HO/Golden Knights/Texas A&M/Daemmrich); iStockphoto: 44 (Tim Fan);
U.S. Air Force photo: 45.

Library of Congress Cataloging-in-Publication Data
Francis, Sandra.
  George Bush / by Sandra Francis.
     p. cm. — (Presidents of the U.S.A.)
  Includes bibliographical references and index.
  ISBN 978-1-60253-069-0 (library bound : alk. paper)
  1. Bush, George, 1924– —Juvenile literature. 2. Presidents—United States—
Biography—Juvenile literature. I. Title. II. Series.

E882.F728 2008
973.928092—dc22
  [B]

2008002303

George Bush thought it was important to "tell the truth, be honest, work hard, try to see the other guy's point of view while sticking to your own principles."

TABLE OF CONTENTS

A PRIVILEGED CHILDHOOD

George Herbert Walker Bush became president after Ronald Reagan left office in 1989. He was the first vice president since Martin Van Buren to be elected to the presidency at the end of his vice presidential **term.** When Bush took office, he faced many difficulties. The U.S. government had the greatest deficit in American history. A deficit is when the amount of money spent is greater than what is in a budget. The American people hoped their new president would lead the country out of debt.

Throughout his presidency, Bush struggled with Congress to get them to agree to less government spending and to adopt new ways of handling other **domestic** problems facing the country. In matters of foreign affairs, however, Congress usually supported him fully. He displayed great skill in relations with

George Herbert Walker Bush was the nation's 41st president.

other countries. President Bush's honesty and efforts in handling of the Persian Gulf War impressed many Americans, but it would not be enough to help him win another election. He held office for just one **term.**

George Bush was born in Milton, Massachusetts, on June 12, 1924. His family moved soon after, and George grew up in Greenwich, Connecticut. His father, Prescott Bush, was a wealthy businessman. Prescott also served as a U.S. senator. George, his three brothers, and their sister were raised in a strict but loving home. Religion was an important part of their

George Bush grew up in a wealthy family that enjoyed many advantages. Even so, he believes his biggest privilege was having parents who loved him. This photo shows Bush (on the left) with his mother, father, sister, and one of his three brothers.

Dorothy Bush chose George's long name in honor of her father. She could not decide which part of her father's name to give her son, so she used the whole thing. He became George Herbert Walker Bush. Grandfather Walker was nicknamed "Pop." Soon people began calling George "Little Pop" and then "Poppy." Today he often uses "Pop" when signing letters to his family.

Barbara's father, Marvin Pierce, was a distant relative of Franklin Pierce, the nation's 14th president.

lives. Prescott Bush taught his children "duty, service, and discipline." George's mother, Dorothy Walker Bush, taught them manners, respect for others, and good sportsmanship. A fine athlete in her own right, Dorothy passed her talents on to George. Throughout his school years, he was especially good at soccer and baseball.

The Bush children enjoyed many privileges. For one thing, they were able to attend the best schools. George attended the respected Phillips Academy in Andover, Massachusetts. The Bush children also enjoyed spending their summers at Walker's Point, on the southern coast of Maine. Their grandfather, George Herbert Walker, owned Walker's Point. He also owned a lobster boat, the *Tomboy*. George and his older brother, Prescott, spent many wonderful days on the *Tomboy*. They developed a love for the open sea.

In December of 1941, just six months before his graduation from Phillips Academy, George met the girl of his dreams. At a Christmas dance, a friend introduced him to Barbara Pierce from Rye, New York. She was the daughter of a magazine publisher. She and George danced and talked all evening. By the following summer, their affection for each other had turned into a lasting relationship. George and Barbara became secretly engaged when she visited the Bush family at Walker's Point. The two were still teenagers, so they would not marry for several years.

After graduating from Phillips Academy, George ignored his school counselor's advice to go to college.

The United States had entered World War II in December of 1941, and George believed it was his duty to join the military and serve his country first. On June 12, 1942, his 18th birthday, George became a seaman in the U.S. Navy. He dreamed of becoming a pilot and soon found himself headed for North Carolina to begin flight training. George became a pilot within one year. When he earned his wings in June of 1943, he was the youngest pilot in the U.S. Navy.

The Bush family spent its summers in Kennebunkport, Maine. George's grandfather owned a large estate there called Walker's Point (above). It was there that George developed a lifelong love for the sea. Today his family still spends as much time as possible at Walker's Point.

George Bush joined the navy shortly after finishing high school. Although his school advisors suggested he go straight to college, George wanted to serve his country first. When he became a pilot, he named his airplane Barbara III, *in honor of the girl he left back home.*

Following intense training, George was assigned to active duty with a torpedo **squadron.** He and his squadron headed for the Pacific. His new home was an aircraft carrier, the *San Jacinto.* George and his crew searched for, photographed, and sometimes attacked the enemy. "Operation Snapshot," as it was called, provided information about the location of destructive Japanese weapons. This was very dangerous work. George had to fly low while another crew member took pictures. They had to get out quickly before the enemy could fire at them. George and his crew had many narrow escapes.

To the relief of his family, George arrived home safely on Christmas Eve of 1944. Two weeks later, on January 6, 1945, he and Barbara married in her hometown of Rye, New York. The couple then moved to Virginia Beach, where George accepted his assignment at the Oceana Naval Air Station in Virginia. There he trained other men to become pilots. Later that year, on August 14, the Japanese surrendered, and World War II was finally over. George was discharged from service on September 18, 1945.

When interviewed by the Academy of Achievement, George cited two very important incidents that changed his life.

". . . as I look back on it, that whole experience (WWII) probably shaped my life more than any incident, or any event. . . . I remember when I was shot down in that war. I remember how terrified I was. And it made me feel close to my family, and to God, and to life, and I was scared. . . . Then we lost a child, . . . a four year-old little girl. It had a profound effect on me and on Barbara. . . . Family and friends and faith are what really matters in life."

While in the navy, George Bush flew 58 **combat missions** before he returned home in December of 1944. For his courageous service, the navy awarded him the Distinguished Flying Cross and three Air Medals.

Just two weeks after George returned home from the navy, he married Barbara Pierce on January 6, 1945.

ACTIVE DUTY

George Bush piloted many dangerous missions during his service with the U.S. Navy. The most frightening of all took place on September 2, 1944. Bush and two other crewmen took off from the deck of the San Jacinto. The plane carried bombs and torpedoes, and the crew prepared to attack the enemy on the island of Chichi Jima. But the Japanese were ready to fight back, and Bush's airplane was surrounded by heavy gunfire.

Bush prepared to strike, but suddenly he felt a terrible thud against the side of the plane. Smoke blew into the cockpit. The plane had been hit! Bush and his crew quickly dropped four bombs on the enemy before pulling away. As they reached the sea, Bush ordered the other men to bail out. Then, with smoke blurring his vision, Bush jumped from the plane. Trouble struck when his parachute tore. He quickly unbuckled his gear so that he would not get tangled in the cords of the parachute when he hit the water.

In the terror of the escape, George lost track of the other two crewmen. With an aching head and his arm burning from a wound, he floated for hours before a submarine, the USS *Finback*, arrived to rescue him. The crew hustled George aboard and then quickly took the submarine beneath the water's surface before the Japanese could spot it. A crew member of the USS *Finback* took the photograph above as George was being rescued. Unfortunately, George later learned that the other two crewmen from his plane had not survived.

CHAPTER TWO

THE BEST OF TIMES

With the end of World War II, happy times were ahead for George and Barbara. "We were still young, life lay ahead of us, and the world was at peace. It was the best of times," recalled George. The newlyweds settled in New Haven, Connecticut, near Yale University. George could now pursue his education, at Yale, and begin family life. While living there, Barbara gave birth to their first child, George Walker, on July 6, 1946. The young couple had no idea that they now had two future U.S. presidents in their family. Not only would George H. W. Bush become the 41st president; their firstborn, George W. Bush, would follow in his footsteps.

Meanwhile, Bush balanced his home life and his studies at Yale. Still a good athlete, he was captain of the school's baseball team. He played in the first NCAA College World Series. As an outfielder, he didn't have the best

Bush's life at Yale was fast-paced and busy. He played for the baseball team, studied, and joined clubs.

11

The Bushes are shown here soon after they moved to Odessa, Texas. From left to right are Barbara, George W., George, Dorothy Bush, and Prescott Bush.

batting average. But his teammates knew that if a ball came his way, he would catch it.

Bush majored in economics, the study of how people use money, goods, and services. In 1948, he graduated with honors, less than three years after he had started college. Bush had a family to support and was anxious to begin his career. It would have been easy to stay in Connecticut and take advantage of his father's business connections, but George and Barbara decided to make it on their own.

The Bushes moved to Texas, where George hoped to start a career in the oil business. He accepted a sales position at a company called IDECO. He spent more than two years learning the business. Next he teamed up with his good friend, John Overbey. Together, with some help from Bush's family, they formed the

Bush-Overbey Oil Development Co. Bush-Overbey purchased the right to look for oil or minerals on people's land. It was a risky business project. If there turned out to be no oil on the land, the company would make no money. Fortunately, they managed to earn a small **profit.** In 1953, with two other oilmen, they formed a new company called Zapata Petroleum. The following year, they started yet another new company, Zapata Off-Shore.

Bush was very successful. He and Barbara had the security they desired for their family. They moved to Houston to be closer to the company's headquarters. In the late 1950s, Bush began to talk with friends about his growing interest in **politics,** the work

After George Walker, Barbara and George Bush had five more children: Robin, John ("Jeb"), Neil, Marvin, and Dorothy.

Bush (far left) dreamed of achieving success in the oil business. By 1954, he had helped start three successful oil companies. Here he is shown examining equipment on an oil rig in the 1950s.

*While Bush's business life was going strong, tragedy struck his family. He and Barbara's young daughter, Robin (right), was diagnosed with **leukemia**, a type of cancer. At the time, there was little hope for people with leukemia. Even the best doctors could not save her. Robin died in 1953—she was almost four years old.*

George and Barbara Bush moved 29 times in 40 years.

of the government. Many Texans belonged to the **Democratic Party.** The Bush family, however, had always been members of the **Republican Party**—the opponents of the Democrats. Bush's friends suggested that he change parties if he wanted to win an election. Instead, he and his supporters began to build up the Republican Party in the county where he lived. George served as chairman of the Harris County Republican Party for two years.

In 1964, Bush ran for a seat in the U.S. Senate but lost. He wasn't discouraged, however. He sold his part of the oil business so he could devote all of his attention to politics. Other Republicans noticed Bush's leadership qualities and gave him their support. With their backing, he won election to the House of Representatives in 1966 and again in 1968. With a background in economics and business, he was a natural to serve on the Ways and Means Committee. This committee helps decide how the government spends its money.

From 1971 to 1977, Bush held many government positions under Republican presidents Nixon and Ford. He served as the U.S. **ambassador** to the

Bush was elected to the House of Representatives twice, but he also lost elections to the U.S. Senate twice—once in 1964 and again in 1970.

In 1966, George Bush won a seat in the U.S. House of Representatives. Here he and Barbara are shown celebrating on election night.

As the U.S. Ambassador to the United Nations, Bush attended many meetings at the U.N. headquarters in New York City.

United Nations in 1971 and 1972. Bush understood the important role of the United Nations. This international organization, made up of more than 180 countries, was founded to end war and achieve world peace.

Although Bush wanted to keep his position with the United Nations, President Nixon asked him to take charge of the Republican National Committee. Bush accepted the position. About that time, President Nixon was accused of wrongdoing in what became known as the Watergate **scandal.** Members of the Republican Party, with Nixon's knowledge, had stolen documents from the Democratic Party. This threatened to destroy Nixon's career—and those of many other Republican politicians.

Bush, as chairman of the party, wrote the following words to President Nixon: "Dear Mr. President, It is my considered judgment that you should now **resign** . . . I now feel that resignation is best for the country. . . . This letter is much more difficult because of the gratitude I will always feel toward you." Bush believed that it was vital for the country to know that the Republican National Committee had nothing to do with the scandal.

After Nixon resigned, Vice President Gerald Ford became president. He chose Bush to head the U.S.

George Bush meets with President Richard Nixon in the Oval Office of the White House.

When Gerald Ford became president, he considered choosing Bush as his vice president. He selected Nelson Rockefeller instead.

Liaison Office in the People's Republic of China. In September of 1974, George, Barbara, and their dog, C. Fred Bush, boarded a plane for Beijing. The job turned out to be limited, but the Bushes made the most of their time in China.

After a year and a half, President Ford asked Bush to return to Washington, D.C. Ford wanted him to head the **Central Intelligence Agency** (CIA). George and Barbara did not look forward to this assignment. The CIA had earned a bad reputation in recent years. Many of its employees were unhappy as well. But while Bush was head of the CIA, he was able to restore **morale** within the agency and regain worldwide respect for the organization.

While in China, George and Barbara rode bicycles like the local people instead of traveling in limousines.

"EVERYBODY'S GRANDMOTHER"

Barbara Bush is a devoted wife and the mother of six children. She is also one of the most admired of all the first ladies. Barbara has said that people like her because "I look like everybody's grandmother."

In June of 1990, Mrs. Bush was asked to speak at the graduation ceremony of Wellesley College, a school for women. Some students there objected to the selection of Mrs. Bush as the speaker. "Barbara Bush has gained recognition through the achievements of her husband," they said. "Wellesley teaches us that we will be rewarded on the basis of our own merit, not on that of a spouse."

Even though not everyone was happy to greet her, Mrs. Bush received a warm welcome at the ceremony. In her speech, she shared her thoughts and ideas with the young women. "At the end of your life, you will never regret not having passed one more test, not winning one more verdict, or not closing one more deal. You will regret time not spent with a husband, a friend, a child, or a parent. . . . One does not need to be married, one does not need to have children. But if you do have children, they must come first." She added that she considers herself the "luckiest woman in the world."

Although Mrs. Bush puts her family first, she has devoted herself to helping people all over the country. She believes one of the most urgent problems in America is illiteracy, the inability to read. She organized the Barbara Bush Foundation for Family Literacy to help people learn to read. She has done much to help other people as well, including the homeless, people with AIDS, and the elderly.

Today the Bushes live in Houston, Texas. They spend their vacations at Walker's Point with their five living children and 14 grandchildren.

CHAPTER THREE

AMERICA'S VICE PRESIDENT

Over the years, Bush had gained valuable knowledge and experience in the workings of the United States government at home and abroad. When he resigned from the CIA in 1977, he was asked to advise several large corporations and was active in various community activities. During this time, he also became a professor at Rice University. Old friendships and political connections in Texas were renewed and Bush began considering the possibility of running for president. "I went home to Texas and started thinking, 'Well why not? I'd like to think I can help make things better, here and abroad."

In May of 1979, Bush announced that he wanted to be the Republican **candidate** for president. He ended his announcement by quoting the words of President Dwight Eisenhower, promising "a leadership confident of our strength, compassionate of heart, and clear in mind, as we turn to the great tasks before us."

To become the candidate, Bush had to win the Republican **nomination.** The contest for the

nomination was between Bush and Ronald Reagan, the governor of California.

After a lively campaign, it was clear that Reagan was going to win the nomination. Reagan asked Bush to be the vice-presidential candidate. Bush answered, "I'd be honored, Governor." They were good partners and easily won the election of 1980. They would win the next election in 1984 as well.

On March 30, 1981, about two months after Reagan became president, the nation was shocked to learn that Reagan had been shot. He was seriously wounded and rushed to the hospital. Bush learned

As director of the CIA, George Bush sometimes met with President Ford.

Ronald Reagan (sitting on desk at left) and George Bush made an excellent team during Reagan's eight years as president.

of the shooting while on a plane to Austin, Texas. He ordered that the plane return to Washington immediately. There he spoke with confidence to the American people, "I can reassure this nation and the watching world that the American government is functioning fully and effectively." Bush handled the crisis with dignity and calm until Reagan returned to duty less than two weeks later.

Bush had made his fortune in the oil industry. But as vice president, he encouraged people to begin using other kinds of fuel instead of gasoline, which is made from oil. Using other fuels would reduce the pollution caused by gasoline. It would also provide additional sources of fuel if oil became scarce.

Vice President Bush was also concerned about the rising use of illegal drugs in the United States. In 1981,

Barbara Bush wrote books about two of her dogs, C. Fred and Millie. The books, *C. Fred's Story: A Dog's Life* and *Millie's Book,* have raised money for the many causes Mrs. Bush supports.

While he was vice president, Bush bought Walker's Point from the rest of his family. He enjoyed life in Maine, spending time playing golf and fishing.

One of the vice president's jobs is to **preside** *over the U.S. Senate. The leader of the House of Representatives is called the speaker of the house. Here, Vice President Bush and Speaker of the House Tip O'Neill chat before President Reagan's 1982 State of the Union address.*

President Reagan put him in charge of the South Florida Task Force. Smugglers from other nations often brought drugs into the United States through Florida. The purpose of the task force was to stop the flow of drugs through that part of the country. Bush quickly brought together many different law-enforcement agencies. He wanted them to work together to stop the drug trade. It was a good first step, but more needed to be done in the countries where the drugs were produced.

In 1988, as Reagan's second term was coming to an end, Bush decided to run for president. He won the nomination, but the race for the White House was not easy. He announced that Dan Quayle from Indiana would be the vice-presidential candidate. Many people thought this was a mistake. Quayle was young and inexperienced. He often made embarrassing speaking blunders. **Debates** were held between the Republican and Democratic candidates. Bush and his Democratic opponent, Michael Dukakis, sometimes seemed boring. Quayle's ignorance and poor choice of words were no match for the sharp wit of Lloyd Bentsen, the Democratic candidate for vice president. Neither Bush nor Dukakis gave Americans a clear idea of what they

In the 1984 election, the Democrats selected a woman named Geraldine Ferraro as their vice-presidential candidate. She was the first woman to receive this honor.

*While he was vice president, Bush met with leaders of **minority groups**. He hoped to improve life in the United States for all Americans.*

The election of 1988 was close, but Bush and Quayle won with 54 percent of the vote.

planned to do for the country. The American public was left to wonder what choices they had.

In the weeks before the election, the issues became more clear. Bush promised he would not raise **taxes,** saying, "Read my lips. No new taxes." This may have helped him win the election, but he would later be forced to break his promise.

With the campaign behind him, Bush could put his vast experience to work for the country. He declared to his advisors, "This is going to be an open presidency. I want you all to feel free to call me at any time; I'm going to call you." At his **inauguration** on January 20, 1989, before 300,000 people, Bush spoke of a "new breeze that would sweep the nation."

The Bush family ran the 1988 presidential campaign from Maine. After a hard day's work, George and Barbara entertained advisors with backyard barbecues at Walker's Point.

As president, George Bush signed into law the Americans with Disabilities Act. This law guarantees the rights of people with disabilities.

CHAPTER FOUR

THE PRESIDENCY

With the Democrats in control of Congress, President Bush was forced to go back on his promise of "no new taxes." The Democrats believed that more taxes would help relieve the national debt. When, finally, Bush gave in and agreed to the tax increases, his fellow Republicans became angry with him. He lost some of the support of his own **political party** and was never able to regain their confidence. He continued to struggle with the nation's **economy** and the Congress throughout his term in office.

President Bush thanks supporters during a Republican Party dinner.

Although Bush had difficulty achieving his domestic goals for the United States, his experience in foreign affairs advanced U.S. leadership around the world. He met with South African leaders to organize a way to end **apartheid,** the system of laws that separated black people from white people in that country. In 1989, he had ordered troops into Panama to capture General Manuel Noriega. General Noriega was a **dictator** involved in his country's drug trade. He was brought to the United States and convicted of sending illegal drugs to other countries.

As Bush entered office, **communist** governments throughout Europe began to collapse. The people of these nations wanted to change their system of government. They began to build **democracies,** governments similar to that of the United States. Germany was one of these nations. Since the end of World War II, it had been divided into two countries. In 1961, when a wall was built separating the German city of Berlin into two parts, it came to symbolize the dividing line between

As the wife of the vice president, and then as the first lady, Barbara Bush had the honor of placing the star atop the national Christmas tree 12 times.

President Bush hated broccoli. Farmers sent the vegetable to the president, hoping to convince him to try it again.

When George Bush took office, he said to the nation, "I see history as a book with many pages—and each day we fill a page with acts of hopefulness and meaning. The new breeze blows, a page turns, the story unfolds."

Since 1961, the Berlin Wall had symbolized the division between communism and democracy. In 1989, during Bush's presidency, the Cold War came to an end. People in Berlin celebrated joyously (above) when the Berlin Wall came down. People even took pieces of the wall as souvenirs.

communism and democracy. In 1989, the Berlin Wall came down, and the two nations became one.

At the same time, the Soviet Union, a communist superpower, began to change its government. Like President Reagan before him, Bush had many meetings with the leader of the Soviet Union, Mikhail Gorbachev. Since the end of World War II, the two countries had had a difficult relationship that became known as the **Cold War.** During this time, the Soviet Union wanted to spread communism around the world. The United States was committed to stopping it. Both nations began to develop and gather dangerous **nuclear weapons.** For decades, it seemed the tense relations between the two countries could develop into a terrible war.

While Bush was in office, the Cold War came to an end. In August of 1991, he and Gorbachev signed the Strategic Arms Reduction **Treaty** (START I). For the first time, the Soviets and Americans agreed to destroy some of their nuclear weapons. In 1992, President Bush and Boris Yeltsin, Russia's new president, signed another treaty, further reducing the number of weapons in both nations. (The Soviet Union dissolved in 1991, and a large portion of it became known officially as Russia.)

In August of 1990, Bush responded to Iraq's invasion of Kuwait. He organized more than 30 countries to stop Iraq and its leader, Saddam Hussein. Congress agreed to cooperate with Bush. It gave him full power to go to war if necessary. War began on January 16, 1991. The United States led its allies in the successful defeat of Iraq. Many Americans praised Bush for his quick and successful operation.

Bush helped begin new peace talks between Israel and Arab countries in the Middle East. For years, Israel had been battling its Arab neighbors. Bush withheld a loan of $10 billion to Israel until it

George and Barbara Bush spent Thanksgiving Day of 1990 with U.S. troops stationed in Saudi Arabia.

*Bush was forced to **compromise** with Congress throughout his four years as president.*

THE PERSIAN GULF WAR

One of the greatest challenges of Bush's presidency was the Persian Gulf War. Saddam Hussein, the dictator of Iraq, wanted to control the world's oil supply. He took steps to invade two oil-rich countries, Saudi Arabia and Kuwait. Hussein planned to take over these two countries—and all of their oil. When his forces invaded Kuwait on August 2, 1990, Bush acted quickly to stop him. He brought together allied forces from 30 countries. He ordered the U.S. military to prepare a huge number of soldiers for combat. Congress gave President Bush its full approval for these actions. The United States and its allies gave Iraq a deadline to leave Kuwait: January 15, 1991.

The plan to stop Iraq became known as "Operation Desert Storm." After months of trying to force Hussein to retreat, war finally broke out on January 16, 1991. For more than a month, aircraft bombed Iraqi military targets. Still Hussein would not give up. On February 23, allied troops marched into Kuwait City to force the Iraqis out. By February 27, Iraq was defeated, and the war soon ended.

Some people criticized Bush for stopping the war before Hussein was removed from power, but the U.S. goal was to return control of Kuwait to the Kuwaiti government. With the experience and knowledge of General Norman Schwarzkopf, head of the allied forces (shown above with President Bush), the plan was completed successfully.

agreed to stop its citizens from settling on Arab lands. This helped him to gain the cooperation of Israel's new leader, Prime Minister Yitzak Rabin.

Bush also signed a trade agreement with Canada and Mexico. The result was the North American Free Trade Agreement (NAFTA) of 1992. The agreement gradually removed taxes to encourage trade between the North American countries. Although Americans admired Bush's success in foreign relations, they were still worried about domestic problems and the economy. Crime was increasing around the country. Unemployment had increased. The national debt was at an all time high.

Even so, Bush easily won the Republican nomination to run in the election of 1992. Democrat Bill Clinton won

Bush was encouraged by the fall of communism around the world. "Out of these troubled times a new world order can emerge," he said. He looked to the future as an "era in which the nations of the world, east and west, north and south, can prosper and live in harmony." He is shown here signing a treaty with Soviet leader Mikhail Gorbachev.

In 2001, George H.W. Bush became the first president since John Adams to be the father of another president. He is shown here with First Lady Laura Bush; his son, President George W. Bush; and his wife, Barbara.

the election, however. "It hurt a lot," recalled Bush. "But the minute we got back to Houston, Texas, and were welcomed by our neighbors, and went into that little house with two dogs and Barbara and me and no one else, we began to say, 'Hey, life's pretty good.'"

Since leaving the White House, the Bushes have had the pleasure of watching two of their sons succeed in politics. In 1994, George was elected governor of Texas. He was reelected in 1998, and his brother Jeb was elected governor of Florida that same year. As the year 2000 rolled around, the Bush family found themselves on the campaign trail again. This time, their son, Governor George W. Bush, won the Republican nomination for president, and then narrowly won the election. He was reelected as president in 2004.

In their golden years, George H. W. and Barbara Bush have remained very active. The Bushes have visited foreign countries and hosted foreign visitors to the United States. To celebrate his 80th birthday in 2004, the former president even went skydiving. Looking back, George H. W. Bush said he was happy with his presidency. When asked what he wished historians would say about him as president, George Bush answered, "He did his best. Did it with honor."

The United Kingdom's Queen Elizabeth II granted the honorary title of Knight Grand Cross of the Order of the Bath to three U.S. presidents: Dwight D. Eisenhower (before he became president), Ronald Reagan, and George H. W. Bush.

George Bush celebrated his 80th birthday with a parachute jump over Texas A&M University. He was accompanied by the U.S. Army Golden Knights parachute team.

BUSH AND CLINTON GIVE BACK

In an interview, George H. W. Bush once said, "The American Dream means giving it your all, trying your hardest, accomplishing something. And then I'd add to that, giving something back. No definition of a successful life can do anything but include serving others."

On December 26, 2004, the opportunity to give back came on the tail of the most powerful earthquake in 40 years. It caused a tsunami, a huge wave that claimed the lives of 275,000 people in Indonesia, the Maldives, Sri Lanka, and Thailand. It is estimated that another nearly 1 million people were flooded out of their homes. Worldwide help was needed.

President George W. Bush responded by requesting that his father and former President Bill Clinton form a partnership to raise funds to aid the victims of the tsunami. In a short period of time, they were able to acquire donations from more then 14,000 contributors, mostly from Houston, Texas. Other donations came from sports organizations: the Houston Texans, Houston Rockets, Houston Astros, the PGA Tour, and Major League Baseball. Their efforts to raise money expanded across the nation, and U.S. citizens gave generously.

The Bush and Clinton team were called upon again when Hurricane Katrina battered the Gulf Coast of the United States on August 29, 2005. More than 1,800 people died, and heavy rains caused flooding and power outages that endangered thousands more people throughout the region. Thousands of people lost their homes and businesses. On September 1, 2005, President George W. Bush requested that the two former presidents come together again to create the Bush-Clinton Katrina Fund. It raised money for the relief and reconstruction of the city of New Orleans and communities in Mississippi and Alabama. Their joint effort raised millions of dollars to assist those affected by the terrible storm.

1920	1940	1950	1960	1970

1924
George Herbert Walker Bush is born in Milton, Massachusetts, on June 12. The family moves to Connecticut shortly after his birth.

1942
Bush graduates from Phillips Academy, in Andover, Massachusetts. On his 18th birthday, he enlists in the U.S. Navy.

1943
Bush becomes the youngest pilot in the U.S. Navy.

1945
Bush marries Barbara Pierce on January 6. The Japanese surrender in August, ending World War II. Bush leaves the navy in September.

1948
Bush graduates from Yale University. He, Barbara, and their son George move to Odessa, Texas, where Bush accepts a job with IDECO.

1951
The Bush-Overbey Oil Development Company is formed in Midland, Texas.

1953
Bush and his business partners found Zapata Petroleum. The Bushes lose their daughter Robin to leukemia.

1954
Bush and his business partners found Zapata Off-Shore.

1959
The Bushes move to Houston where George runs Zapata Off-Shore.

1963
Bush is elected chairman of the Harris County Republican Party.

1964
Bush loses election to the Senate.

1966
Bush is elected to the U.S. House of Representatives.

1968
Bush is reelected to the House of Representatives.

1970
Bush again runs for the Senate, but loses.

1971
Bush is sworn in as the U.S. ambassador to the United Nations.

1973
Bush becomes chairman of the Republican National Committee.

1974
President Ford appoints Bush chief of the U.S. Liaison Office in the People's Republic of China. George and Barbara Bush move to Peking.

1976
Bush is appointed director of the Central Intelligence Agency (CIA).

1980
Bush is elected Ronald Reagan's vice president.

1981
John Hinckley attempts to assassinate President Reagan. Bush takes over the duties of the president during Reagan's two-week recovery.

1984
Bush and Reagan are reelected.

1988
Bush is elected the 41st president of the United States. Dan Quayle is his vice president.

1989
Bush is inaugurated on January 20. President Bush has his first meeting with Soviet leader Mikhail Gorbachev. Bush sends troops to Panama to capture dictator Manuel Noriega, who is involved in his country's drug trade. The Berlin Wall comes down, reuniting East and West Germany.

1990
Bush signs the Americans with Disabilities Act. Iraq invades Kuwait in August. Bush prepares to stop the invasion.

1991
On January 16, the Persian Gulf War begins when Bush gives orders to begin Operation Desert Storm to drive Iraqi invaders out of Kuwait. Kuwait is liberated in late February. Bush orders an end to combat in the Persian Gulf. Together with Soviet leader Mikhail Gorbachev, Bush signs the Strategic Arms Reduction Treaty (START I), a treaty to reduce nuclear weapons in the two countries. Gorbachev later resigns from his position, and the Soviet Union dissolves.

1992
Bush and Quayle lose the election. Canada, Mexico, and the United States sign the North American Free Trade Agreement to encourage trade between the three countries.

1993
Before leaving office, Bush and the Russian president, Boris Yeltsin, sign START II, banning the most dangerous nuclear weapons. George and Barbara Bush return to private life in Houston after President Bill Clinton enters office.

1994
George and Barbara's oldest son, George W. Bush, is elected governor of Texas.

1997
The George Bush Presidential Library, located at Texas A&M University, is dedicated.

1998
George W. Bush is reelected governor of Texas. John Ellis "Jeb" Bush is elected governor of Florida.

2000
George W. Bush is elected president of the United States after a close election.

2004
On June 12, George H. W. Bush goes skydiving in honor of his 80th birthday.

2005
On January 3, former presidents George H.W. Bush and Bill Clinton agree to lead the national campaign to raise money to aide the victims of the Indian Ocean tsunami.

2005
August 31, the Bush and Clinton Katrina Fund was established to aid the victims of Hurricane Katrina.

2007
Bush received the Ronald Reagan Freedom Award, an award given to "those who have made monumental and lasting contributions to the cause of freedom worldwide," and to those who "embody President Reagan's lifelong belief that one man or woman truly can make a difference."

GLOSSARY

allied forces (AL-eyed FOR-sez) Allied forces are military troops from different countries that come together to fight a common enemy. Bush brought together allied forces from 30 countries during the Persian Gulf War.

ambassador (am-BASS-eh-der) An ambassador is an important representative sent by one country to another. The United States sends ambassadors to other countries, as well as to the United Nations.

apartheid (uh-PART-hite) Apartheid is a political policy in which people of different races are kept apart from one another. President Bush worked to help end apartheid in South Africa.

candidate (KAN-dih-det) A candidate is a person running in an election. Bush hoped to be the Republican presidential candidate in 1980.

Central Intelligence Agency (SEN-truhl in-TEL-ih-juhnz AY-juhn-see) The Central Intelligence Agency (CIA) is a government agency that collects information about people, businesses, and foreign governments to protect the United States. Bush served as director of the CIA.

Cold War (KOHLD WOR) The Cold War was a period in history, from the 1950s to about 1991, during which the United States and the Soviet Union greatly distrusted each other. The Cold War was not an actual war, but a time when it seemed that war could erupt at any time. The Cold War ended during Bush's presidency.

combat missions (KOM-bat MISH-uhns) Combat missions are missions to capture or defend something. As a navy pilot during World War II, Bush flew 58 combat missions.

communist (KOM-yeh-nist) In a communist country, the government, not the people, holds all the power, and there is no private ownership of property. The Soviet Union was a communist country.

compromise (KOM-pruh-myz) To compromise is to settle a disagreement by both sides giving up part of what they want. Bush compromised with Democrats in Congress.

debates (deh-BAYTZ) Debates are formal discussions on a topic between two or more people. Before an election, candidates participate in debates to express their views.

democracies (deh-MOK-ruh-seez) Democracies are nations in which the people control the government by electing their own leaders. The United States is a democracy.

Democratic Party (dem-uh-KRAT-ik PAR-tee) The Democratic Party is one of the two major political parties in the United States. The Democratic Party opposed George Bush's party, the Republican Party.

dictator (DIK-tay-tur) A dictator is a ruler with complete power over a country. Saddam Hussein was the dictator of Iraq during the Persian Gulf War.

domestic (duh-MESS-tick) Domestic refers to matters at home or within the country. Bush and Congress could not agree on solutions for the domestic problems of the United States.

economy (ee-KON-uh-mee) An economy is the way money is earned and spent. Bush struggled with the nation's economy while he was president.

inauguration (ih-nawg-yuh-RAY-shun) An inauguration is the ceremony that takes place when a new president begins a term. Bush's inauguration took place on January 20, 1989.

leukemia (loo-KEE-mee-uh) Leukemia is a disease in which the blood makes too many white blood cells. Bush's daughter Robin died of leukemia.

liaison (lee-AY-zahn) A liaison is a person or group that works to establish friendly relations between two parties. Bush worked at the U.S. Liaison Office in China.

minority groups (mye-NOR-uh-tee GROOPS) Minority groups are people of a certain race, ethnic group, or religion that are a small group within a larger population. Bush met with minority groups to hear their concerns.

morale (mor-AL) Morale is the attitude or spirit of a group. Bush was able to restore morale within the CIA.

nomination (nom-ih-NAY-shun) If someone receives a nomination, he or she is chosen by a political party to run for office. To become the Republican Party's presidential candidate, Bush needed to win the nomination.

nuclear weapons (NOO-klee-ur WEH-punz) Nuclear weapons use energy to cause powerful explosions, which result in terrible destruction and death. Bush and Soviet leader Mikhail Gorbachev signed a treaty to reduce the number of nuclear weapons in their countries.

political party (puh-LIT-ih-kul PAR-tee) A political party is a group of people who share similar ideas about how to run a government. Bush lost some support from members of his political party when he raised taxes.

politics (PAWL-uh-tiks) Politics refers to the actions and practices of the government. Bush became interested in politics in the late 1950s.

preside (preh-ZYD) When people preside over something, they are in charge of it. The vice president presides over the Senate.

profit (PRAH-fit) A profit is money that is left over after all of the expenses of running a business are subtracted from the total amount of money earned. When it first started out, the Bush-Overbey Oil Development Company earned a small profit.

Republican Party (re-PUB-lih-kin PAR-tee) The Republican Party is one of two major political parties in the United States. George H. W. Bush is a member of the Republican Party.

resign (ree-ZYN) When people resign, they give up a job or position. The Watergate scandal forced President Nixon to resign.

scandal (SKAN-dul) A scandal is a shameful action that shocks the public. The Watergate scandal involved President Nixon.

squadron (SKWAD-run) A squadron is a group of military units. While in the navy, Bush was assigned to a torpedo squadron.

taxes (TAK-sez) Taxes are payments of money made by citizens to support a government. During the 1988 election, Bush promised there would be no new taxes while he was president.

term (TERM) A term is the length of time a politician can keep his or her position by law. A U.S. president's term of office is four years.

treaty (TREE-tee) A treaty is a formal agreement between nations. In 1991, Bush and Soviet leader Mikhail Gorbachev signed the Strategic Arms Reduction Treaty to reduce the number of weapons each country had.

tsunami (tsoo-NAH-mee) A tsunami is an unusually large sea wave caused by an underwater earthquake or volcano. It can cause great destruction and take many lives. Parts of Asia were hit by a devastating tsunami on December 26, 2004.

United Nations (yoo-NYE-tid NAY-shuns) The United Nations is an international organization set up to promote world peace and cooperation. Bush served as U.S. Ambassador to the United Nations.

THE UNITED STATES GOVERNMENT

The United States government is divided into three equal branches: the executive, the legislative, and the judicial. This division helps prevent abuses of power because each branch has to answer to the other two. No one branch can become too powerful.

EXECUTIVE BRANCH

PRESIDENT
VICE PRESIDENT
DEPARTMENTS

The job of the executive branch is to enforce the laws. It is headed by the president, who serves as the spokesperson for the United States around the world. The president signs bills into law and appoints important officials such as federal judges. He or she is also the commander in chief of the U.S. military. The president is assisted by the vice president, who takes over if the president dies or cannot carry out the duties of the office.

The executive branch also includes various departments, each focused on a specific topic. They include the Defense Department, the Justice Department, and the Agriculture Department. The department heads, along with other officials such as the vice president, serve as the president's closest advisers, called the cabinet.

LEGISLATIVE BRANCH

CONGRESS
Senate and
House of Representatives

The job of the legislative branch is to make the laws. It consists of Congress, which is divided into two parts: the Senate and the House of Representatives. The Senate has 100 members, and the House of Representatives has 435 members. Each state has two senators. The number of representatives a state has varies depending on the state's population.

Besides making laws, Congress also passes budgets and enacts taxes. In addition, it is responsible for declaring war, maintaining the military, and regulating trade with other countries.

JUDICIAL BRANCH

SUPREME COURT
COURTS OF APPEALS
DISTRICT COURTS

The job of the judicial branch is to interpret the laws. It consists of the nation's federal courts. Trials are held in district courts. During trials, judges must decide what laws mean and how they apply. Courts of appeals review the decisions made in district courts.

The nation's highest court is the Supreme Court. If someone disagrees with a court of appeals ruling, he or she can ask the Supreme Court to review it. The Supreme Court may refuse. The Supreme Court makes sure that decisions and laws do not violate the Constitution.

CHOOSING
THE PRESIDENT

I t may seem odd, but American voters don't elect the president directly. Instead, the president is chosen using what is called the Electoral College.

Each state gets as many votes in the Electoral College as its combined total of senators and representatives in Congress. For example, Iowa has two senators and five representatives, so it gets seven electoral votes. Although the District of Columbia does not have any voting members in Congress, it gets three electoral votes. Usually, the candidate who wins the most votes in any given state receives all of that state's electoral votes.

To become president, a candidate must get more than half of the Electoral College votes. There are a total of 538 votes in the Electoral College, so a candidate needs 270 votes to win. If nobody receives 270 Electoral College votes, the House of Representatives chooses the president.

With the Electoral College system, the person who receives the most votes nationwide does not always receive the most electoral votes. This happened most recently in 2000, when Al Gore received half a million more national votes than George W. Bush. Bush became president because he had more Electoral College votes.

THE WHITE HOUSE

The White House is the official home of the president of the United States. It is located at 1600 Pennsylvania Avenue NW in Washington, D.C. In 1792, a contest was held to select the architect who would design the president's home. James Hoban won. Construction took eight years.

The first president, George Washington, never lived in the White House. The second president, John Adams, moved into the house in 1800, though the inside was not yet complete. During the War of 1812, British soldiers burned down much of the White House. It was rebuilt several years later.

The White House was changed through the years. Porches were added, and President Theodore Roosevelt added the West Wing. President William Taft changed the shape of the presidential office, making it into the famous Oval Office. While Harry Truman was president, the old house was discovered to be structurally weak. All the walls were reinforced with steel, and the rooms were rebuilt.

Today, the White House has 132 rooms (including 35 bathrooms), 28 fireplaces, and 3 elevators. It takes 570 gallons of paint to cover the outside of the six-story building. The White House provides the president with many ways to relax. It includes a putting green, a jogging track, a swimming pool, a tennis court, and beautifully landscaped gardens. The White House also has a movie theater, a billiard room, and a one-lane bowling alley.

PRESIDENTIAL PERKS

The job of president of the United States is challenging. It is probably one of the most stressful jobs in the world. Because of this, presidents are paid well, though not nearly as well as the leaders of large corporations. In 2007, the president earned $400,000 a year. Presidents also receive extra benefits that make the demanding job a little more appealing.

★ **Camp David:** In the 1940s, President Franklin D. Roosevelt chose this heavily wooded spot in the mountains of Maryland to be the presidential retreat, where presidents can relax. Even though it is a retreat, world business is conducted there. Most famously, President Jimmy Carter met with Middle Eastern leaders at Camp David in 1978. The result was a peace agreement between Israel and Egypt.

★ *Air Force One*: The president flies on a jet called *Air Force One*. It is a Boeing 747-200B that has been modified to meet the president's needs.

Air Force One is the size of a large home. It is equipped with a dining room, sleeping quarters, a conference room, and office space. It also has two kitchens that can provide food for up to 50 people.

★ **The Secret Service:** While not the most glamorous of the president's perks, the Secret Service is one of the most important. The Secret Service is a group of highly trained agents who protect the president and the president's family.

★ **The Presidential State Car:** The presidential limousine is a stretch Cadillac DTS.

It has been armored to protect the president in case of attack. Inside the plush car are a foldaway desk, an entertainment center, and a communications console.

★ **The Food:** The White House has five chefs who will make any food the president wants. The White House also has an extensive wine collection.

★ **Retirement:** A former president receives a pension, or retirement pay, of just under $180,000 a year. Former presidents also receive Secret Service protection for the rest of their lives.

FACTS

QUALIFICATIONS

To run for president, a candidate must

- ★ be at least 35 years old
- ★ be a citizen who was born in the United States
- ★ have lived in the United States for 14 years

TERM OF OFFICE

A president's term of office is four years.
No president can stay in office for more than two terms.

ELECTION DATE

The presidential election takes place every four years on the first Tuesday of November.

INAUGURATION DATE

Presidents are inaugurated on January 20.

OATH OF OFFICE

I do solemnly swear I will faithfully execute the office of the President of the United States and will to the best of my ability preserve, protect, and defend the Constitution of the United States.

WRITE A LETTER TO THE PRESIDENT

One of the best things about being a U.S. citizen is that Americans get to participate in their government. They can speak out if they feel government leaders aren't doing their jobs. They can also praise leaders who are going the extra mile. Do you have something you'd like the president to do? Should the president worry more about the environment and encourage people to recycle? Should the government spend more money on our schools? You can write a letter to the president to say how you feel!

1600 Pennsylvania Avenue
Washington, D.C. 20500
You can even send an e-mail to: president@whitehouse.gov

BOOKS

Childress, Diana. *George H. W. Bush*. Minneapolis: Twenty-First Century Books, 2007.

Davis, Marc. *George Herbert Walker Bush*. Minneapolis: Compass Point Books, 2003.

Foster, Leila Merrell. *The Story of the Persian Gulf War*. Chicago: Children's Press, 1991.

Greene, John Robert. *The George H. W. Bush Years*. New York: Facts On File, 2006.

Warren, James A. *Cold War: The American Crusade against the Soviet Union and World Communism, 1945–1990*. New York: Lothrop, Lee & Shepard, 1996.

VIDEOS

The American President. DVD, VHS (Alexandria, VA: PBS Home Video, 2000).

The Gulf War. VHS (Alexandria, VA: PBS Home Video: 1996).

The History Channel Presents The Presidents. DVD (New York: A & E Home Video, 2005).

National Geographic's Inside the White House. DVD (Washington, D.C.: National Geographic Video, 2003).

INTERNET SITES

Visit our Web page for lots of links about George Bush and other U.S. presidents:

http://www.childsworld.com/links

Note to Parents, Teachers, and Librarians: We routinely verify our Web links to make sure they are safe, active sites—so encourage your readers to check them out!

INDEX